RAD
AMERICAN
WOMEN
A-Z

WRITTEN BY
KATE SCHATZ

ILLUSTRATED BY
MIRIAM KLEIN STAHL

CITY LIGHTS BOOKS
SAN FRANCISCO

Cover and interior design: Jason Pontius

Printed in The United States

Library of Congress Cataloging-in-Publication Data

Schatz, Kate.
Rad American women A-Z / written by Kate Schatz;
illustrated by Miriam Klein Stahl.
_____ pages cm
ISBN 978-0-87286-683-6
1. Women—United States—Biography—Juvenile literature.
I. Klein Stahl, Miriam, illustrator. II. Title.
CT3260.S33 2015
920.72—dc23

2014037930

City Lights Books are published at the City Lights Bookstore,
261 Columbus Avenue, San Francisco, California 94133.
www.citylights.com

RAD AMERICAN WOMEN A-Z

For Hazel, Ivy, and Benson

And for X

WELCOME TO *RAD AMERICAN WOMEN A-Z!*

American history is filled with stories of brave and powerful men . . . but have you ever wondered where the women are? In this book you will find the stories of 26 women who have made a big impact on our nation.

They represent different races and ethnicities and come from different parts of the country. Some grew up very poor, and some had rich families. Some were born long, long ago, and some are still living. There are artists and sports heroes, rock stars and scientists.

What do they have in common? Every single one of these individuals changed America in some way. Each one worked hard and believed in herself, even when others expressed doubt or said no. These rad women have all said, "Yes I can."

What does it mean to be "rad"? Well, it means a few things. "Rad" is short for "radical," which comes from the Latin word meaning "from the root." So a radical person can be someone like Ella Baker, who did grassroots organizing. A radical can be a person who wants to make big changes in society, like Angela Davis and the Grimke sisters, who fought to end discrimination of all kinds. Radical can also be used to describe something that is different from the usual, like Maya Lin's Vietnam Memorial or Ursula LeGuin's innovative science fiction. "Rad" is also a slang word that means "cool" or "awesome." Like when flashy Flo-Jo ran faster than any woman in the world, or when Patti Smith takes the stage to rock out.

We hope that you find inspiration in these pages, whether you're a girl or a boy or a parent or a teacher! These women are American heroes, and they're part of all of our histories. We can find inspiration in the stories of all people, no matter who they are. And no matter who you are, you can make a difference, too.

Enjoy the book! Love,

Kate (the author!) & Miriam (the illustrator!)

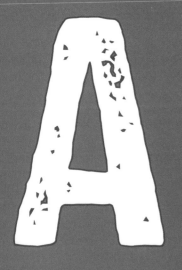

A
IS FOR
ANGELA

ANGELA DAVIS

Who never backs down from the fight for justice

Angela Davis was born in 1944 in Birmingham, Alabama, into a neighborhood known as "Dynamite Hill" because a group of racist white men called the Ku Klux Klan often bombed the homes of black families who lived there.

Schools were segregated in Alabama back then, and the education that black children received was inferior by far. Despite those difficulties, Angela was a smart and curious child, and her parents were thrilled when she got a scholarship to a high school in New York City, where she could go to school safely and pursue her passion for learning.

Angela thrived in her new school, and she and her new friends attended rallies and protests in support of the Civil Rights movement, which demanded equal rights for black people in America. In college she was one of only three black students in her class. She felt isolated, but she didn't let that stop her from learning. Angela loved philosophy and literature, and she continued her college career in Europe, where she studied the writing of many great thinkers. She connected their ideas with her own beliefs about the injustice that she was witnessing.

She began speaking out against racism and sexism, and in favor of gay rights. She criticized the U.S. government for its role in the Vietnam War. In 1969 she was hired as a college professor, but the Governor of California had her fired because of her political beliefs. Her students and fellow teachers were outraged, and they rallied to support Angela. She didn't get that job back, but she went on to teach at several other prestigious universities, and she continued to speak out about injustice, wherever it occurred.

Today, Angela educates people about the unfair treatment of prisoners. She has written nine books, including a book about her own life. She is a powerful and inspiring public speaker, and people listen to Angela because she is a strong black woman who is never afraid to tell the truth, to speak her mind, and to demand justice and liberation for all people.

B

IS FOR
BILLIE JEAN

BILLIE JEAN KING

Who showed the world what female athletes can do

Billie Jean King was 12 years old when she had her first tennis lesson, and she knew right away that she wanted to play tennis for the rest of her life. By 1973, she was the top female tennis player in the world, and had won more than 30 Grand Slam titles.

When a former tennis champ, Bobby Riggs, challenged her to "The Battle of the Sexes"—a contest to prove who was better at tennis, men or women—she refused at first. She wanted to concentrate on being the best tennis player she could be, and didn't want to be distracted by some name-calling guy. But Riggs kept challenging her, bullying her in public with sexist teasing. Eventually, Billie Jean decided she just had to play in the contest. "I thought it would set us back 50 years if I didn't win that match," she said. "It would affect all women's self-esteem."

When the day came, more than 30,000 people packed the Houston Astrodome to watch, and millions around the world tuned in on their TV sets to see if a woman could really beat a man at tennis. And beat him she did!

Billie Jean won three sets in a row, and at the same time won the respect of the whole world. Her victory gave women's sports a huge boost because it showed people that women could be athletic and strong, and that they could compete with men.

But Billie Jean didn't stop there. After the "Battle" she continued to play professional tennis. And she was one of the first professional athletes to publicly acknowledge that she is gay, which was a brave step, since discrimination against gay people still exists, and it can hurt their careers. She was inducted into the Tennis Hall of Fame, and in 2009 President Obama awarded her the Presidential Medal of Freedom in honor of all the work she has done for women and for the gay and lesbian community.

C IS FOR CAROL

CAROL BURNETT

Who showed us that funny women can make it big

There wasn't much to laugh about during Carol Burnett's childhood, but she managed anyhow, thanks to her great imagination and quirky sense of humor.

Carol was born in Texas in 1933, and her parents were both alcoholics who got into lots of fights. When she was 8 she went to live with her grandmother, "Nanny," in a one-room apartment in a run-down part of Hollywood, California. When Nanny was able to scrape together enough money, she'd treat Carol to a trip to the movies. And that's when Carol fell in love with the silver screen.

She wanted to go to college to study playwriting, but they didn't have the $42 to pay for the school. Then one day an envelope containing a $50 bill magically appeared in her grandmother's mailbox, and off to college Carol went. She never found out who left the money, but she was always grateful.

At college, Carol decided to take an acting class. She got up on stage, and she realized something special: She was funny! Her classmates laughed and laughed, and it made her feel good. "All of a sudden, after so much coldness and emptiness in my life, I knew the sensation of all that warmth wrapping around me," she once explained. Carol had always been a shy, quiet girl, but in that moment, everything changed.

Carol moved to New York and found work in musicals and cabaret shows, and eventually on television. Even though everyone loved her, Carol's TV bosses were shocked when she asked for her very own variety show. Back then, variety shows were the most popular shows on TV, and only men hosted them. But Carol insisted, and "The Carol Burnett Show" was born. It was a smash success, and at the end of every show she would smile at the camera and tug on her left ear. This was a secret signal to her beloved Nanny, who was watching back home, to let her know that everything was OK.

"The Carol Burnett Show" was on TV for 11 years and won more than 25 awards, making Carol famous, and a role model for women in comedy and television.

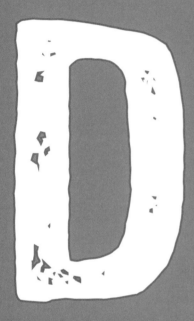

D

IS

FOR

DOLORES

DOLORES HUERTA

Who demands dignity and justice for farm workers

Dolores Huerta was raised in Stockton, California, by a hardworking single mother. Dolores was an excellent student, and after she graduated from high school she became an elementary school teacher.

Many of her students were the children of farm workers, the people who plant and harvest the fruit and vegetables that end up on our dinner tables. They worked hard in the fields but made very little money, and Dolores's students suffered from the effects of poverty, often coming to school without shoes. The conditions for farm workers were terrible—they couldn't leave work to go to a doctor, weren't allowed to take bathroom breaks, and didn't even have clean water to drink. Dolores loved teaching, but she felt she could do more to help her students if she could help their parents. She became a community organizer, working to help the farm workers win some basic human rights.

She soon met César Chávez, another activist, and together they created a union called the United Farm Workers Association. A union is an organization that helps protect the rights of people who have the same kind of job. This union asked people all across the land to stop eating grapes until the men and women who picked the fruit were treated more fairly. Soon, the United States government made laws to protect the farm workers, and Dolores was recognized as one of the most important leaders of American workers. She helped people all over the country earn a living wage and have healthier, safer lives.

Dolores made a difference off the fields as well, by fighting sexism within her own community. One day, at a meeting of other important leaders, she decided to write down every insulting comment about women that she heard. At the end, she told the men in the group, "During the course of this meeting, you guys have made 58 sexist remarks." Many of the men were surprised— they hadn't even realized the rude things they were saying! During the next meeting, Dolores counted 30 sexist comments. Slowly but surely, the men changed their ways, until there were zero offensive comments. By speaking up and demanding that her peers talk respectfully, Dolores reminded them that everyone deserves to be treated with dignity and kindness.

E IS FOR ELLA

ELLA BAKER

Who shaped the Civil Rights movement from behind the scenes

Ella Baker was one of the most important people in the Civil Rights movement, but she's not the most famous. And that's how she liked it.

Ella learned about racism and cruelty at an early age; her grandmother had been born a slave, and she told Ella about how she was whipped for refusing to marry the man her master had chosen for her. Ella admired her grandmother's courage.

After college, Ella moved to New York and became involved with several organizations working to support women, African Americans, and workers. She was an excellent leader, but she didn't want to be in the spotlight; she wanted to work in the background, teaching ordinary people how to make a difference. Ella believed that for real change to happen, people needed to come together in organized ways to talk about their goals and plan their actions. Many people think that famous leaders like Dr. Martin Luther King Jr. and Rosa Parks worked alone, but they were part of large groups of people who worked hard to plan the marches, rallies, sit-ins, and other activities that were key to the success of the Civil Rights movement in America.

Ella Baker worked with both Dr. King and Rosa Parks, and she helped start two of the most important groups of the time: the Southern Christian Leadership Conference and the Student Nonviolent Coordinating Committee. Ella was a leader in the National Association for the Advancement of Colored People, and she also helped young white students join with black people in the fight for civil rights. This was a time when most political leaders were men, but that didn't stop Ella.

Her grandmother's courage and strength were major inspirations to Ella throughout her life, whether she was telling the Mayor of New York City why black and white children should go to school together; organizing sit-ins in restaurants that didn't allow black people inside; or helping people register to vote during the Mississippi Freedom Summer. Ella was called "the backbone of the Civil Rights movement," but she was also a big part of its heart.

F

IS FOR

FLO-JO

FLORENCE GRIFFITH-JOYNER

Who showed us how to run like a girl

One day in school, Florence Griffith's teacher asked her what she wanted to be when she grew up. "Everything," she said. "I want to be everything."

The other kids laughed. No one expected much from Florence, who lived with her mom and 10 siblings in a housing project. But she knew she was unique and fabulous, even if her peers did not. She loved colorful clothes and did her hair in all kinds of cool styles.

Florence was also incredibly fast, something her family realized when she was young. Since it wasn't safe to roam around the neighborhood, she and her siblings spent their time playing a variety of sports. Florence always won. At age 7 she started competing in track competitions, and at 14 she won the Jesse Owens National Youth Games. She broke her high school records in sprints and the long jump, and she also got straight A's. She dreamed of greatness, and of a gold medal.

Florence competed on the track team in college and won many races. Her coaches believed she could be an Olympic star. But times were tough, and she felt she needed to help support her family, so she dropped out of school and got a job as a bank teller. Her coach knew she was too good to give up on her dream, and he helped her get financial aid to return to school and the team. And it was worth it.

Florence trained harder than ever, and in 1984 she competed in the Olympics, where she won a silver medal in the 200-meter dash. She designed her own outfits, including bright one-legged bodysuits. Reporters started calling her "Flo-Jo" because of her flashy style.

In 1988, at the Olympic Trials, Flo-Jo set a new world record for the 100-meter dash, and later at the Olympics she won three gold medals and a silver one. She became the Fastest Woman in the World, and her record in the 100-meter dash is still unbroken.

G IS FOR THE GRIMKE SISTERS

THE GRIMKE SISTERS

Who devoted their lives to the pursuit of freedom and equality for all

Angelina and Sarah Grimke were sisters who were born 12 years apart, but they were like twins when it came to their commitment to ending slavery.

In the early 1800s, the Grimke family lived in Charleston, South Carolina, on a fancy cotton plantation. Like most other rich white families in the South, the Grimkes owned slaves. The sisters saw their daily suffering and knew it wasn't right. Even though it was against the law, Angelina secretly taught one of their slaves to read. She and Sarah tried to convince their parents that slavery was wrong, but Mr. and Mrs. Grimke wouldn't listen. So the girls made a hard but powerful decision: They said goodbye to their parents, their 11 siblings, and the fancy dresses and dances. Then they moved north to Philadelphia, where the anti-slavery movement was beginning.

The Grimke sisters joined the Quakers, a religious group dedicated to nonviolence, and they became abolitionists (people working to end slavery). They gave passionate speeches and wrote fiery letters in support of freedom for all people. They didn't care if people tried to punish or persecute them for their convictions. "Emancipation," Angelina wrote, "is a cause worth dying for!" The pro-slavery people were furious at the sisters, and some of their fellow Quakers were shocked that a woman should say such things. Some angry people even burned their articles and letters!

Not everyone was upset, though. Many people admired Sarah and Angelina. They traveled to more than 67 cities, giving speeches to mixed audiences of men and women, blacks and whites together. In their lectures they explained that the equality of women was connected to the freedom of black people. Again, people were outraged, because they had never heard white women express these kinds of ideas. Many abolitionist men failed to support equality for women, and many early feminists did not care about ending slavery.

In 1838 Angelina became the the first American woman to speak in front of a legislative body when she presented anti-slavery petitions signed by 20,000 women to the Massachusetts Legislature. Sarah and Angelina lived and worked together for their entire lives, united in their belief that all human beings deserve freedom and equality.

H

IS FOR HAZEL

HAZEL SCOTT

Whose many talents helped her blaze a bright trail

One day, when Hazel Scott was a very little girl, she walked up to the piano and began to play a church hymn. Hazel hadn't been taught to play the piano yet, and her mother, a piano teacher, watched in awe as Hazel played every note perfectly.

After Hazel's parents divorced, her mother brought her talented daughter from their home in the island nation of Trinidad and Tobago to America. When she was only 8 years old, Hazel tried out for the Juilliard School of Music. She was way too young—you had to be 16 to get in—but her mother convinced them to let her audition. Her performance was so impressive that she was offered a scholarship. Hazel was a musical genius, they said.

Her career took off from there. Hazel's style combined classical music with jazz, blues, and swing, and she could sing in seven languages. She went to school during the day, and in the evenings she was the hottest act at the best nightclubs in New York City. Soon she was acting on Broadway, and in 1950 she became the first African American to host her own television show, "The Hazel Scott Show."

Even though Hazel was famous, she still had to face racism in her life and in her career. A strong, outspoken woman, she never hesitated to speak up about injustice. She refused to play for any segregated audience, and when she became a movie star she challenged the way Hollywood treated non-white people. She demanded to be paid the same as white actors, and refused to play roles that were demeaning to black people.

Her strong beliefs made her a hero to many, but she also became a target for something called the House Committee on Un-American Activities, a group of paranoid politicians who put Hazel on their list of suspected Communists. Even though she appeared before their committee to defend herself, they "blacklisted" her, which means they told people not to hire her. Her popular TV show was cancelled, and she moved to Paris, where she lived and played jazz music for many more years. Hazel never backed down from her principles, and remained true to her amazing talent.

IS FOR

ISADORA

ISADORA DUNCAN

Who showed us the power of imagination and originality

Dreamer. Rebel. Free spirit. Visionary. Isadora Duncan was all of these, and more. With her flowing costumes, innovative ideas, and graceful movements, Isadora invented a new style of dance.

Isadora Duncan was born into an artistic but troubled San Francisco family. After her parents' divorce she moved with her mother and siblings to Oakland, California. Life was hard, and though Isadora dropped out of school at a young age, she loved to read and learn. She spent hours at the Oakland Public Library, reading books recommended by the librarian (who happened to be a famous poet, Ina Coolbrith.)

Isadora took ballet, but she didn't like the rigid positions and uncomfortable shoes. She preferred to make up her own dances, inspired by the world around her. She would go to the beach and use her body to imitate waves, flying birds, and wind. To earn money, Isadora and her sister taught dance classes to neighborhood children. The classes—and Isadora's style—became increasingly popular, and soon they taught in San Francisco, too. But Isadora, always a dreamer, wanted more.

She and her family moved to Chicago, and then to New York City. Young Isadora performed her bold dances on many stages. Everything about her performance was new and different, from her movements to her bare feet to the way she breathed while she danced. While some people loved it, many Americans did not. It was too different for them, too strange! Some people thought that her sheer, flowing costumes were inappropriate. Others weren't used to seeing female dancers who weren't ballerinas.

So the rebellious Isadora headed to Europe, where she found audiences able to appreciate her work. She quickly became a sensation. She performed in many European countries, and was able to bring her mother and siblings over to live with her, too. She never lost her passion for teaching, and once she became famous she opened several dance schools for girls, where she spent her days teaching other creative young women how to dance from their hearts and follow their dreams, too.

J IS FOR JOVITA

JOVITA IDAR

Who believed in free and equal education for all children

Jovita Idar was many things during her lifetime, including a nurse, a journalist, an editor, and a political activist. She was also a teacher who believed that all children had the right to a good education, no matter how much money their parents had or what language they spoke.

Jovita, the oldest of eight children, was born in 1885 in Laredo, Texas, a town on the Texas/Mexico border. Her father ran a newspaper called *La Crónica* that published articles in Spanish, many of which spoke out against the prejudice experienced by the Idars and many other families who were Mexican and Tejano (Texans of Spanish or Mexican heritage). Jovita wrote for the paper, but she also wanted to be a teacher. At 17 she got her teaching credential and began to teach in Los Ojuelos, a tiny town on the border, not far from Laredo. Her students were poor and the school was in terrible shape. It had no heat, no textbooks, and not enough desks and chairs. Jovita asked for more funding for her school, but the education leaders in Texas refused to listen to her. Poor Mexican American students were not a priority for them.

This made Jovita furious, but it also inspired her to take action. "Mexican children in Texas need an education," she said. "There is no other means to do it but ourselves!" She organized a group of women called La Liga Femenil Mexicanista (Mexican Feminist League). They taught poor children and adults how to read and write, and created bilingual lessons to be used in schools. They also opened new schools, including one in Los Ojuelos that had heat and textbooks. These schools were free and open to all children.

And that wasn't all Jovita did. After she published an article that criticized President Woodrow Wilson for sending soldiers to the U.S./Mexico border, the Texas Rangers showed up at the newspaper office to try to shut it down! Jovita stood in the doorway to block them from entering and to defend her freedom of speech. Soon after that, her father passed away, and Jovita took over *La Crónica*. She became the editor-in-chief and spent many more years as a courageous and influential journalist.

K

IS FOR

KATE

KATE BORNSTEIN

Who reminds us to bravely claim our true identity

Kate Bornstein was born a healthy baby boy named Albert in 1948. Her parents raised her just like all the other boys in their small New Jersey town. But Kate knew early on that something wasn't right: She just didn't feel like a boy.

Kate wasn't comfortable wearing boy clothes or doing boy things. But she didn't know what to do. What would she tell her parents? What would the kids at school say? She kept her secret to herself for a long time. She was relieved when she discovered her talent for theater during college, because acting in plays allowed her to pretend to be other people. Kate loved acting, and she began to write and act in her own plays. She got married and had a daughter, but she still struggled with her identity.

Your "sex" refers to the body parts that you're born with, and your "gender" is more about how you feel. Some people are born with male body parts, but they feel like women. Some are born with female parts but they feel like men. And some people don't feel like either. Kate realized that she was "transgender," which means that she doesn't identify as the sex she was born with. She believes that we should have more than just those two choices of gender. Many cultures throughout history have believed this same thing, too.

Kate knows that life can be hard when you don't fit in, especially when you're a young person. She wants to help put an end to bullying, and she believes one of the best ways to do this is to educate and support young people of all genders. She has spent much of her life writing books and plays about these complicated issues. Her books are taught in schools all over the world and have been translated into five languages.

Kate likes to call herself an "outlaw" because she lives in a way that's different from what people consider "normal." She doesn't apologize for who she is or how she lives, and she wants other young outlaws to love themselves, too.

L

IS FOR

LUCY

LUCY PARSONS

Who fought for the rights of workers and poor people

Lucy Gonzalez Parsons was born in Texas during the Civil War era. She was of Native American, Mexican, and African American ancestry. Little is known about her early years, but her parents might have been slaves.

When she grew up, Lucy married a white man named Albert Parsons, even though it was against the law for people of different races to get married in Texas. After Albert faced violent threats for helping former slaves register to vote, they knew they had to leave the state.

The couple moved north to Chicago, where men were building railroads, homes, and roads, and women were working in factories. Lucy watched as poor people worked long hours, desperately trying to make enough money to feed their families, while the wealthy people who owned the factories and railroads lived comfortable lives. Lucy and Albert joined organizations that aimed to improve conditions for workers. Strong-willed Lucy led meetings, wrote articles, and gave speeches. She also gave birth to two children, and after Albert was fired from his job because of his political activism, she opened her own dress shop to support the family.

On May 1, 1886, Lucy and her family helped lead a march of 80,000 people down the streets of Chicago. They wanted to pass a law that would guarantee workers an eight-hour workday, because there were no limits to how many hours a person was expected to work. Sometimes people were forced to work for 16 hours straight! A few days later, Albert gave a peaceful speech at another rally. When the police came, it turned violent. Albert was arrested, and this became known as the Haymarket Riot. Lucy led the campaign to defend her husband; she traveled around the country and gave 43 speeches in 17 states. The police followed her everywhere, waiting for her outside the meeting halls to try to stop her from speaking. The Chicago police once said she was "more dangerous than 10,000 rioters"!

In the end, Lucy wasn't able to free her husband, but she never gave up her crusade for justice. Lucy spent her life speaking out and writing about workers' rights, racism, and women's issues, fighting to make America a fair place for all.

M

IS FOR

MAYA

MAYA LIN

Who makes big ideas into beautiful art

Maya Lin's parents came to America from China just before Maya was born. As a child she loved to play by herself, using her imagination as she explored nature and played in her dad's ceramics studio.

Maya got straight A's in school and excelled at math and science. She especially liked to build models of miniature towns, so it made sense when she decided to become an architect.

When Maya was still a student at Yale University, she entered a contest to design a memorial for the American soldiers who had died serving in the Vietnam War; it would be built in Washington, D.C., for all to see. Maya submitted her unique design, but didn't think she would win. She was only 21 years old, after all, and her design was very different from the other grand memorials that had been constructed in the nation's capital. The Vietnam War was very controversial, and Maya wanted her design to show that. Instead of a statue, Maya imagined a big, shiny wall covered in the names of soldiers. The wall would reflect the image of the person looking at it, like a mirror. That way, Maya thought, visitors would see themselves in the wall of names, and be reminded that war affects us all.

More than a thousand people entered the contest, and Maya—a college student—won! This upset some people, but Maya defended her design and refused to back down when several politicians demanded she change it. She believed in her work and saw it through—and now the Vietnam Veterans Memorial is one of the most frequently visited memorials in the United States.

That's not all Maya has done. She continues to work as an artist, making giant sculptures inspired by natural landscapes and science. She is passionate about the environment, and sometimes she uses garbage and recycled materials, including her children's old toys, to make art. She has also designed parks and other memorials, including the Civil Rights Monument in Montgomery, Alabama.

N

IS FOR

NELLIE

NELLIE BLY

Who changed the face of journalism—and world travel

Nellie Bly's real name was Elizabeth Cochrane, but as a famous writer and adventurer she was known as Nellie. No matter what she was called, one thing was for sure: She was a rebel who knew how to write!

Nellie was born in 1864. After her father died, she had to work to help support her family. She loved to write, and she always read the *Pittsburgh Dispatch* newspaper. The most popular column was written by a man who called himself the Quiet Observer, or "Q.O." He said that women who worked outside the home were "a monstrosity." This infuriated Nellie! She wrote an angry letter to the paper—and guess what? Her letter was so well-written that the *Dispatch* offered her a job. Her editor picked the pen name "Nellie Bly" for her, after a popular song.

She wrote her first article about poor working girls in Pittsburgh. She loved to investigate her topics and learn as much as she could. She even traveled to Mexico on her own and worked as a foreign correspondent. But the editors kept asking her to write about fashion and flowers. Fed up, Nellie left them a note and headed to New York City. The note said, "Dear Q.O., I'm off for New York. Look out for me. Bly."

Nellie was only 23 when a famous New York editor asked her to write about a mental institution. She didn't just write about it—she pretended to be ill and stayed at Blackwell's Island for 10 days! The story she wrote exposed the cruel treatment of patients. It also got the attention of politicians, who made reforms to improve the hospital. Nellie became well-known as a journalist who exposed corruption and celebrated the working class. She even interviewed Susan B. Anthony, a famous leader in the struggle for women's right to vote.

In 1889 Nellie set off on an epic adventure: to beat Phileas Fogg, the fictional hero of the book *Around the World in Eighty Days*. She packed one dress, a few pairs of underwear, a coat, and a small bag of toiletries. Her solo voyage around the world was made on ships, trains, and even a donkey. She finished her journey in 72 days, 6 hours and 11 minutes, and returned to New York to cheering crowds. She had set a world record!

O IS FOR ODETTA

ODETTA

Who led the way with her powerful voice

When Odetta Holmes was 7 years old her family moved from Birmingham, Alabama, to Los Angeles, California, in search of a better life.

It was 1937, and the Great Depression had hit them hard. While they were on the train headed west, they were told to leave the car they were in and move to another one because they were black. Odetta never forgot this cruel moment.

In high school Odetta trained as a classical singer and performed musical theater. She was very talented, and people thought she would become a famous opera star. But then she went to San Francisco and heard folk music being played in coffeeshops. Unlike the opera arias she had studied, the folk songs told stories that Odetta could relate to. She began to combine folk music with the blues and gospel she'd grown up with, performing her songs in clubs in New York and San Francisco.

Her big, powerful voice and strong stage presence amazed people, and she quickly developed a following. At the time, most folk singers were white, and many of them were male. Odetta defied this stereotype and toured around the country. During the 1950s she recorded several popular albums and became one of the best-known folk singers in the country.

As the 1960s began, Odetta and her music became more political, and she began to be involved in the Civil Rights movement. Dr. Martin Luther King called her the "Queen of American Folk Music," and she performed at the 1963 March on Washington, singing a song called "O Freedom" for the huge crowd of protesters who had come to the U.S. capital to demand equality for all.

Odetta sang at many other important rallies and protests, and even performed for several Presidents. Her inspiring songs helped bring people together as they fought to end racial prejudice and discrimination. When Rosa Parks was once asked which songs meant the most to her, she replied, "All of the songs Odetta sings."

P

IS FOR

PATTI

PATTI SMITH

Who put the poetry in punk rock

When she was young, Patti Smith didn't seem much like a future rock star. She was shy, skinny, and awkward, and often sick. Despite all that, she believed in herself.

Patti loved all kinds of art: She listened to jazz and rock music, read poetry, and learned about artists like Picasso. She was inspired by them, and knew she wanted to make art, too. "When I was a little kid, I always knew that I had some special kind of thing inside me," she remembers.

Patti tried working at a regular job, and she tried going to college, but her creative dreams were too powerful to put on hold. She moved to New York City in 1967 and started hanging out with photographers, painters, playwrights, and musicians. It was an exciting and creative time. Patti and her new friends made art together, and she often shared her poetry. But she didn't just read her poems—Patti was loud and bold, and she used her body and her voice to communicate emotions. She started performing her poems while her friend Lenny played guitar, and eventually she began to sing. She started a band, and people packed into clubs to see this new kind of music called punk rock.

Punk rock was like rock 'n roll, but louder and more messy and fun. The guitars were wild, the drums were fast, and the performers were sweaty and thrilling. And like rock 'n roll, punk was dominated by men—but not when Patti was onstage. She would fearlessly wail and howl her words into the microphone. When she jumped and danced she was no longer the shy, sickly, scrawny kid she'd once been. She was the powerfully creative artist, expressing herself with every word.

Patti has lived her whole life as an artist. Besides writing songs and recording many albums, she's written plays, books of poetry, and a memoir about her life. She has won many awards, and even though she's old enough to be a grandma now, her performances are still filled with wild, inspiring energy.

Q

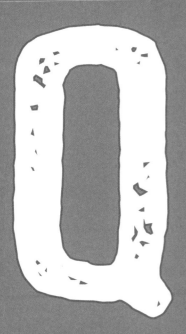

IS FOR QUEEN BESSIE

"QUEEN BESSIE" COLEMAN

Who soared above discrimination

Bessie Coleman was 11 years old and living in Texas when the Wright Brothers completed the first successful airplane flight in 1903. She read stories about these flying machines, and she dreamed of soaring through the air herself.

Bessie's family was very poor, and even though her mother didn't know how to read, she encouraged her daughter to pursue an education. The one-room schoolhouse for African American children was four miles from their home, and on days when Bessie didn't have to pick cotton in the field, she would walk all the way there and back. Despite her hardships, Bessie got good grades and was able to graduate.

As a teenager Bessie continued her hard work. She polished other people's nails, washed their laundry, and served their food. She also listened to the tales that her brothers told her about the female pilots in France who flew planes in World War I. Then she read about Harriet Quimby, the first American woman to get a pilot's license. That was that! Bessie decided she was going to be a pilot. She tried to enroll in aviation schools, but every one of them turned her down. No one would accept a black woman.

Did that stop Bessie from pursuing her dream? No way! She began taking French lessons and soon raised enough money to travel all the way to Paris, all by herself. There, she was finally accepted into a flying school. She was the only black woman, and even after she witnessed a fellow student's terrible plane crash, she kept going. It took her seven months to learn how to fly a plane, and in 1921—two years before Amelia Earhart—she got her international pilot's license.

Bessie continued to train as a stunt pilot, learning how to do crazy tricks like spins, dives, and loop-the-loops. This was called "barnstorming," and Bessie excelled at these daring feats. She performed all over Europe, and back in the United States, too. People called her "Queen Bessie" because she was the best and bravest female pilot out there.

R IS FOR RACHEL

RACHEL CARSON

Who taught us how to respect and protect the Earth

When Rachel Carson was a young girl, she discovered a fossilized seashell buried in a hill on her family's farm. Curious Rachel wanted to know all about it: How old was it? And how did it end up in rural Pennsylvania when the ocean was so far away?

Rachel loved to explore nature, and finding the fossil sparked what she called a "feeling of absolute fascination for everything relating to the ocean." She also loved to write, and her mother encouraged both of these passions. They spent hours exploring the fields and streams near their house, and at home they read book after book. Rachel published her first story when she was only 10 years old.

In college Rachel went on to study writing, marine biology, and zoology. She wrote articles and radio programs about conservation, and she worked as a biologist, researching underwater ocean sounds. She was one of the only women in the whole country doing this kind of work. By 1956 she'd written three books and was credited with introducing the idea of "ecology"—the study of the natural world—to the public.

Rachel is most famous for her last book, *Silent Spring*, which is about the danger of a pesticide called DDT that was being sprayed on plants to control insects. Rachel's research showed that chemicals like DDT were harmful to the environment, even though the companies that made them told the public that they were safe. She knew the book would be controversial, and at first she was scared to write it. But she knew she had to expose the truth.

The makers of DDT did attack her, and she defended her research. *Silent Spring* became a best-seller, and Rachel appeared before Congress to testify about the dangers of pesticides. They listened, and soon DDT was banned. Rachel's passion for nature and her brave commitment to telling the truth helped start the modern environmental movement.

S IS FOR SONIA

SONIA SOTOMAYOR

Who reminds us to be fair and fierce all at once

Sonia Sotomayor was raised in a housing project in the Bronx in the 1950s. Her parents came to New York City from Puerto Rico, where they both had only limited opportunities for education. They didn't speak much English and they worked hard so they could send Sonia and her brother to a good school.

Sonia was very smart. She had perfect attendance and the best grades in the whole school. She was also brave. When she was 7 she was diagnosed with juvenile diabetes, a disease that affects the way your body digests sugar. She had to give herself a shot every day, all by herself.

Even as a child, Sonia always loved the law. She read all the Nancy Drew books and thought of becoming a detective. But then she learned about judges and lawyers, and that changed her mind. "I was going to college and I was going to become an attorney, and I knew that when I was 10," she once said.

Sonia got a full scholarship to Princeton University. She was thrilled, but there were hardly any other Latinos there, and most people came from families with lots of money, nothing like what she knew back in the Bronx. She felt like "a visitor landing in an alien country." At first she felt too intimidated to ask questions during class. But Sonia believed in herself, and knew she deserved to be there. Over time, she became a student leader and activist, and helped convince Princeton to hire more Latino professors and offer courses about Latin American history. At graduation, she was at the top of her class yet again.

Sonia worked as a lawyer for many years, and as an advocate for women and the Puerto Rican community. But her dream was to be a judge. When it happened, Sonia was the first Puerto Rican woman to become a judge in a U.S. federal court. In 2009, President Obama called Sonia to see if she would like to join the Supreme Court, the most important court in the United States. She was so excited that she had to put her hand over her chest to calm her pounding heart! Sonia is the first Latina/o to ever serve on the Supreme Court, and the third female Supreme Court justice in history.

 **IS FOR TEMPLE**

TEMPLE GRANDIN

Who shows us the power of a brilliant mind

Temple Grandin's parents knew she was different when she was still just a baby. She didn't talk, laugh, or make eye contact, and she had enormous tantrums.

Temple reacted strongly to loud sounds, scratchy fabrics, and strong smells. In 1949, when she was only 2 years old, a doctor diagnosed her with autism, a developmental disorder that affects behavior and communication. Everyone knew there was something wrong with Temple, but they didn't realize that a lot was right. Temple's mind was different, but it wasn't damaged . . . it was brilliant!

Temple is a visual thinker. Her mind shows her pictures instead of words. As a child she was an amazing artist, and she loved to design and build things. But talking to people made her uncomfortable, like "an anthropologist from Mars," she says, and she was bullied constantly. She struggled in school—until she finally found something she could relate to.

Once, during a visit to a cattle ranch, Temple felt a deep connection to the horses and cows. She knew that the animals had feelings, but that they couldn't express them with words. This was exactly how she'd always felt herself. Temple realized that autistic people and animals have a lot in common. She started getting ideas for ways that farmers and ranchers could help their animals feel safe and happy. Using her drawing skills and visual mind she started to design pens, walkways, devices, and buildings that would improve the animals' quality of life.

At first, many farmers and ranchers didn't want to work with her. They thought her ideas were strange, and they didn't think an autistic woman could help them. But once they saw how the animals reacted to her, and how well her ideas worked, they started to listen.

Dr. Temple Grandin has written several books, worked as a college professor, and given speeches all around the world. She has dedicated her life to reducing the suffering and anxiety of animals, and to educating people about autism and the mind.

U

IS FOR

URSULA

URSULA K. LeGUIN

Whose books show us that other worlds are possible

Ursula K. Le Guin grew up in Berkeley, California, the child of two well-known anthropologists. Her family home was a gathering place for scientists, students, writers, and all sorts of interesting people.

This was at a time when most young girls were expected to be "seen and not heard," but Ursula's parents thought the opposite. They encouraged their intelligent daughter to ask questions and to learn from their fascinating guests.

Ursula was inspired to write stories. She loved making up imaginary new worlds and creating characters like the ones she read about in Norse mythology, *Alice in Wonderland*, and *The Hobbit*. She submitted her first short story to a magazine when she was 11. It was rejected, but she didn't lose faith in herself and kept on writing. By the time she was in her 20s she had written five novels, but nothing had been published. She still didn't give up. She started writing science fiction because she thought it might be easier to get it published, and she was right! Popular magazines started printing her stories, taking note of this exciting new writer.

In the 1950s and '60s, most science fiction writers were men. Though their work was popular, it wasn't seen as "real literature." People thought their books were just about aliens and robots. Ursula helped change this perception. Like other sci-fi stories, her books describe future worlds, but Ursula also explored important issues like gender, war, and religion in her work. In her novel *The Left Hand of Darkness*, most of the characters have no gender at all. Also, Ursula thought it was wrong that the heroes in sci-fi and fantasy novels were always white, so she made a conscious effort to include a variety of skin colors in her novels. When her publishers tried to put only white people on the covers of her books because they thought they would sell more copies that way, Ursula demanded that they change them.

And Ursula doesn't just write sci-fi. She has published 21 novels, 11 volumes of short stories, four collections of essays, 12 children's books, and six volumes of poetry. She has won many awards, is an inspiration for numerous writers, and has helped millions of readers to imagine the possibilities of the future.

 IS FOR

VIRGINIA

VIRGINIA APGAR

Whose invention saves lives every single day

Virginia Apgar grew up in a creative household. She played violin and cello, and spent time doing experiments with her science-loving dad.

But there was sadness in the home, too. Virginia's oldest brother died of tuberculosis, and another brother suffered from chronic illnesses. This made Virginia determined to become a doctor. With the help of several scholarships she went to college, where she played violin and cello in the orchestra and studied zoology.

Virginia decided she wanted to be a surgeon, which was very rare for a woman at the time. The Great Depression was just beginning, and even though Virginia graduated from medical school at the top of her class, she struggled to find work. Even male surgeons had a hard time getting jobs during the Depression, but it was much harder for a young woman. So Dr. Apgar transferred to a new medical field called anesthesiology. Anesthesiologists are trained to give patients anesthetics, which numb the pain of medical procedures like surgery.

Virginia became especially interested in working with babies and women who were giving birth, and she studied the effects of anesthesia on newborn infants and their mothers. This resulted in her most important invention: the Apgar Score, a simple but important method of evaluating the health of a new baby. One minute after birth, doctors and nurses evaluate and score the infant's breathing, heart rate, muscle tone, reflexes, and overall appearance. They do this again five minutes later. The results are added up: a low Apgar score means that the baby needs help, and a high Apgar score means the baby is healthy. The practice quickly caught on, and it is now used all over the world. Through her research Virginia also discovered that the kind of anesthesia usually given to mothers during labor was unsafe, and thanks to her, doctors stopped using it.

It's been said that Dr. Virginia Apgar has "done more to improve the health of mothers, babies, and unborn infants than anyone else in the 20th century." She went on to become the very first Professor of Anesthesiology in the United States, and is considered a pioneer in many medical fields.

W

IS FOR

WILMA

WILMA MANKILLER

Who led her people with strength and courage

When Wilma Mankiller was growing up, her family's little wooden shack didn't have indoor plumbing, running water, or electricity. What they did have was a strong, close-knit community, and a connection to their Cherokee tribe.

But life was often hard, and a long drought made it impossible to stay on their farm in Oklahoma. In 1956 the Mankillers (whose name came from a powerful ancestor) moved to San Francisco as part of the U.S. government's Indian Relocation Act, which encouraged Native Americans to move from rural to urban areas.

The move was hard on Wilma. She had never seen tall buildings or bright city lights. She'd never even used a phone! They were the only Native Americans in their new neighborhood, and at school Wilma was teased about her name. She felt disconnected from her culture until the late 1960s, when a group of young people took over the tiny island of Alcatraz in the San Francisco Bay. They claimed the island "in the name of Indians of all tribes" to call attention to the government's bad treatment of Native Americans. Visiting the protesters changed Wilma forever. She was inspired to work for change within her community, and she became the director of the Native American Youth Center.

Eventually Wilma returned home with her two daughters to live on her grandfather's land in Oklahoma. She knew that her people faced many challenges, and she wanted to help them solve their problems independently, without the government telling them what to do. She worked to improve health care, education, and access to clean water. Her efforts caught the eye of the tribal Chief, who selected her to be his Deputy Chief. Not everyone was happy about this, as there had never been a woman leader of a Native American tribe. Wilma proved her critics wrong by being an effective and strong leader.

In 1985 she became the first-ever female Chief. She helped her people get jobs, settled many disputes, and increased tribal membership by thousands. Wilma was a wise, bold leader who was loved by her people.

 **IS FOR THE WOMEN WHOSE NAMES WE DON'T KNOW.**

It's for the women we haven't learned about yet, and the women whose stories we will never read.

X is for the women whose voices weren't heard.

For the women who aren't in the history books or the Halls of Fame, or on postage stamps and coins.

For the women who didn't get credit for their ideas and inventions.

Who couldn't own property or sign their own names.

The women who weren't taught to read or write but managed to communicate anyway. Who weren't allowed to work but still supported their families, or who worked all day but weren't paid as much as the men.

X is for the radical histories that didn't get recorded.

X is for our mothers, our matriarchs, our ancestors.
The nurses and neighbors and aunties and teachers.
The women who made huge changes and the women who made dinner.
X is for the hands that built and shared and wrote and fought.
The bodies that birthed and worked and strained to keep going.
The feet that walked, ran, jumped, and balanced.
The minds that dreamed and desired, the hearts that loved.

X is also for all that's happening now and all that is still to come.
X is for the women in homes and offices and fields and labs and classrooms, who invent and transform and build and create.

X is for all we don't know about the past, but X is also for the future.

X marks the spot where we stand today.

What will *you* do to make the world rad?

Y IS FOR YURI

YURI KOCHIYAMA

Who fought for the rights of <u>all</u> people

During the 1930s Yuri Kochiyama was a typical California teenager. She played tennis, taught Sunday school, and loved "the red, white and blue."

Yuri was "Nisei," or second-generation Japanese American. Her immigrant parents, who had come to California from Japan, were "Issei," meaning first-generation. Being Japanese in America was never a problem for Yuri and her family—that is, until December 7, 1941, when Japan bombed a U.S. naval base called Pearl Harbor. That same day, the FBI came to Yuri's house and took her father away because they thought he might be a spy. Yuri's twin brothers volunteered to fight as soldiers in the war, but Yuri and the rest of her family were forced to move to internment camps along with more than 100,000 other Japanese Americans. They were sent all the way to Arkansas, thinking it would only be for a few weeks. They were imprisoned there for three whole years.

Yuri met her husband at the camp. When they were finally released, they moved to New York City, had six children, and lived in housing projects among black and Puerto Rican neighbors. The Civil Rights movement was starting, and Yuri worked in a restaurant with almost all black employees. They told her of life in the segregated South, how even the black soldiers in uniform weren't allowed in restaurants with the white soldiers. Hearing these stories changed Yuri. "I didn't wake up and decide to become an activist," she said. "But you couldn't help notice the inequities, the injustices. It was all around you."

She held meetings in her family's apartment and invited activists to speak about many different causes. Her kitchen table was covered with political pamphlets, and she taped newspaper articles to the walls. She rallied for better schools in Harlem and helped support the movement for Puerto Rican Independence. In 1963, she met the powerful black leader Malcolm X; they became close friends and often worked together. Yuri was fierce and bold, and she defied the stereotypes of Nisei women, who were supposed to be quiet and obedient. She didn't just work for the rights of Japanese Americans, but for the rights of all Americans—black, white, Asian, Latino, and Native. She was a lifelong humanitarian who inspired younger generations of activists.

Z

IS FOR

ZORA

ZORA NEALE HURSTON

Who captured the stories and voices of many generations

Zora Neale Hurston's mother encouraged her children to "always jump at the sun." It was good advice, and it's just what the bold, brash Zora did.

Zora grew up in Eatonville, Florida, the first all-black town in the United States, a place where black people could own businesses and be elected to important positions. Zora loved Eatonville and the people in it. When she wasn't reading books, she was listening to the townsfolk tell colorful stories that had been passed down for generations. Zora absorbed this folklore, and began to make up her own fantastical tales as well.

After her mother died, Zora's life became difficult. For years she drifted around without a real home, working here and there as a maid, but always wanting more. She managed to make her way to Howard University, where she studied theater and joined a literary club. From there she headed to New York City, where she settled in the neighborhood of Harlem. There, she joined thousands of other African Americans who were creating music, art, and literature. This was called the Harlem Renaissance. Zora was charming and outgoing, and quickly befriended great artists like Langston Hughes. She began publishing her stories and plays, most of which were based on the stories and people she remembered from her Southern childhood. It was an exciting time for black artists like Zora, and she was in the center of it all.

A scholarship to Barnard College led the ever-curious Zora to study cultural anthropology. She began traveling the world to record the stories, songs, dances, and voices of black cultures. This kind of research is called fieldwork. She trekked across the American South, Haiti, Jamaica, and Honduras, taking pictures and learning all about these rural communities. She published essays about what she learned and also wrote novels, using her research to create authentic dialogue between her characters, like Janie and Teacake in her novel *Their Eyes Were Watching God*. In all, Zora published four novels, two books of folklore, an autobiography, numerous short stories, and several essays, articles, and plays. She is considered one of the great American writers of the 20th century.

ONE OF THE HARDEST (AND MOST FUN!)

parts of making this book was choosing which people to include. There are only 26 letters in the alphabet, and there are thousands of rad women whose stories deserve to be shared.

They can't all fit in this book—but hey, maybe you can write one too! Draw a picture or make a sculpture of your favorite rad woman. Write your next book report on one. Ask your teachers to tell you about some of their favorite rad women.

Now that you've read about Angela, Zora, and everyone in between, you might be thinking about what you can do to make a difference in the world and your community. Here are a few ideas!

26 THINGS THAT <u>YOU</u> CAN DO TO BE RAD!

ACT as an ally in support of all people.

BELIEVE in yourself and all you can do.

CREATE art: Sing, dance, paint, write!

DARE to be the only one. Only girl on the team? Only boy wearing pink? Cool!

EDUCATE yourself both in school and out. Being smart is rad.

FRIENDSHIP is powerful, and way better than gossip and bullying.

GIVE more than you take. Hugs, gifts, smiles, advice—giving makes us feel good.

HOPE for the best, even when things aren't going great.

INSPIRE others. You can be a hero to people younger than you—and older too!

JOKES are important! Making people laugh can be a powerful tool.

KNOW where you come from. Who are your ancestors? What are their stories?

LISTEN up! Share your thoughts, but listen to what others have to say, too.

MAKE mistakes, learn from them, and keep on trying.

NURTURE the living beings you love.

OUTSIDE can be more fun than inside. Get out and explore!

PROTECT yourself by being safe and making smart choices.

QUESTIONS are awesome. Raise your hand and ask away!

RESPECT the Earth and all its living creatures.

STAND UP for what you believe, and for people who can't stand up for themselves.

TRY new things, even if you're afraid of failure.

UNDERSTAND others. Instead of judging people, try getting to know them.

VOICE your opinions loud and clear, even if you don't think anyone is listening.

WORK together. Teamwork is fun!

X-RAY everything! Learn what's inside.

YOURSELF is the best thing you can be. You don't need to be anyone else.

ZERO tolerance for discrimination! Speak up when you witness unfair treatment.

RESOURCE GUIDE

We used all kinds of sources to research this book. It was so much fun to learn all about American history and the lives of these rad women. Here are some books, websites, and organizations you might want to check out.

BOOKS ABOUT RAD WOMEN

Anderson, Laurie Halse. *Independent Dames: What You Never Knew About the Women and Girls of the American Revolution*. New York: Simon & Schuster Books for Young Readers, 2008.

Bausum, Ann. *With Courage and Cloth: Winning the Fight for a Woman's Right to Vote*. Des Moines: National Geographic Children's Books, 2004.

Bolden, Tonya, ed. *33 Things Every Girl Should Know About Women's History*. New York: Crown Publishers, 2002.

Harness, Cheryl. *Remember the Ladies: 100 Great American Women*. New York: HarperCollins, 2003.

Lunardini, Christine. *What Every American Should Know About Women's History*. Avon: Adams Media Company, 1997.

Mink, Gwendolyn and Marysa Navarro. *The Reader's Companion to U.S. Women's History*. New York: Houghton Mifflin, 1998.

Pinkney, Andrea Davis. *Let It Shine: Stories of Black Women Freedom Fighters*. New York: HMH Books for Young Readers, 2013.

Roehm McCann, Michelle and Amelie Welden. *Girls Who Rocked the World: Heroines from Joan of Arc to Mother Teresa*. New York: Aladdin, 2012.

Thimmesh, Catherine. *Girls Think of Everything: Stories of Ingenious Inventions by Women*. Boston: Houghton Mifflin, 2000.

FURTHER READING ABOUT THE
RAD WOMEN IN THIS BOOK

Borden, Louise and Mary Kay Kroeger. *Fly High! The Story of Bessie Coleman*. New York: Aladdin, 2004.

Butcher, Nancy. *It Can't Be Done, Nellie Bly!: A Reporter's Race Around the World*. Atlanta: Peachtree, 2003.

Fradin, Dennis Brindell and Judith Bloom Fradin. *Zora!: The Life of Zora Neale Hurston*. New York: Clarion Books, 2012.

Jones, Sabrina. *Isadora Duncan: A Graphic Biography*. New York: Hill and Wang, 2008.

Lawlor, Laurie. *Rachel Carson & Her Book that Changed the World*. New York: Holiday House, 2012.

Montgomery, Sy. *Temple Grandin: How the Girl Who Loved Cows Embraced Autism and Changed the World*. New York: Houghton Mifflin Books for Children, 2012.

Warren, Sarah. *Dolores Huerta: A Hero to Migrant Workers*. Seattle: Two Lions, 2012.

Winter, Jonah. *Sonia Sotomayor: A Judge Grows in the Bronx / La juez que creció en el Bronx*. New York: Atheneum Books for Young Readers, 2009.

WEBSITES AND ORGANIZATIONS

A Mighty Girl
www.amightygirl.com

National Organization of Women
www.now.org

National Women's Hall of Fame
www.greatwomen.org

National Women's History Museum
www.nwhm.org

National Women's History Project
www.nwhp.org

PBS 'Makers' Project
www.pbs.org/makers

ACKNOWLEDGMENTS

Kate and Miriam would like to thank:

Jason Pontius; Laura Atkins; Leslie Van Every; Conway & Young; Michelle Tea, Virgie Tovar, and RADAR Productions; Elaine Katzenberger, Stacey Lewis, and everyone else at City Lights.

Miriam also thanks:

Rydell, Gillian and Levi; Finn, Olive and Mabel; Ruby, Nora and Ezra; Coco and Taz; Leah, River, Jasper, Atticus, Hart, Georgia, Lola and Lenny Bruce; Maisy and Johnny; Drew and Ryan; Hannah and Danny; Arts and Humanities Academy students and staff; Bubby and Zaide; The Graces, Nana, Brooke and Billy and the brilliant Lena Wolff.

Kate also thanks:

Ivy Cat and Benson Bowie; Barbara and Doug Schatz; Aubrey Schatz; Nancy Murray; OSA and Literary Arts; and all my rad friends and Facebook brainstormers for their invaluable input and support, especially Kristina, who was so excited for this project.

Visit our website:

radamericanwomen.com